A Pocket Full of Nature

By Rebecca A. Baisden

Printed in The United States of America.

ISBN-13:
978-1535177511

ISBN-10:
1535177519

This book is Dedicated to:

The Child in every one of us who wants to get up, go outside, and play.

And to the Wildlife and Conservation Volunteers who work to preserve and protect this beautiful natural World of ours.

Contents

1.

A Pocket Full of Nature

She has a pocket full of nature.
When she goes outdoors she collects feather, leaves and stones,
She stores them in her treasure chest.
as soon as she gets home.

Her treasure chest is a music box.
It isn't filled with trinkets or jewels,
It holds her natural treasures,
More precious to her than gold.

Each item is a priceless memory;
telling the story of all the hikes she's been on.
Like last year while hiking in Laurel Hill,
when they saw that new born fawn.
She found a spotted leaf,
that reminded her of its fur.
She pressed it for her treasure chest.
Now that moment is preserved.

Her pocket is always full of nature.
She's hiking or exploring all the time.
She loves being out in nature.
She never knows what treasures she will find.

7-7-2016

<u>To Take Flight Through the Night</u>

I close my eyes,
open my arms,
and take flight.

Toes bend over the window sill,
stretch out my wings,
in the late night chill.

With star light to guide me,
soar on past the shore,
out over the open sea.

Skim the waves as I take flight.
Race with the dolphins,
as I fly through the night.

Slowing in the first light of dawn,
circle the morning star,
as the world sleeps on.

Land softly in the dew kissed grass,
feeling tired and proud,
for I have flown at last.

12-5-2005

3.

Little Yellow Bird - Eagle Heart

There is a little yellow bird soaring,
through my back yard.
The way he chases the sparrows and crows,
I guess he thinks he's an Eagle in his heart.

It's amazing to watch him,
The way he darts and dives.
He's not going to let up on them.
He sure is a determined little guy.

He's making the yard his home.
He sweeps in low and swirls about.
The bigger birds don't stand a chance.
The trees are his; Eagle Heart will keep them out.

Well, the yard is clear now.
He's out there all alone.
Singing a sweet little song.
Ah, he's calling his lady love home.

Their sweet songs fill the air,
as the little yellow birds build their nest together.
She has no need to fear a thing,
with her Eagle Heart always keep watch out there.

4-24-2006

4.

Morning

The warmth of the sun heats my face to awaken me;

awareness sneaks upon me without warning.

The aroma of opening flowers entices me to my feet,

with the first breath of morning.

Ah, it's so sweet to be in the mountains,

and catch the world still yawning.

The newness of this beautiful day,

the youth of the morning, touches my heart and I sigh.

I am grateful to greet another day; to be surrounded by nature.

I cherish this golden moment as I hear a young eagle's first cry.

6- 14-1987

5.

<u>One Leaf</u>
One small leaf falling,
Leaving the safety of his mother's limb.
Softly landing upon the caressing surface,
Of a gentle mountain stream.

Floating, freely, peacefully,
down the mountain, finally on his own.
Smiling in the sunlight,
Proud of himself for how much he has grown.

Suddenly, without warning!
He is turning, this way and that,
Crashing into rocks and broken logs.
Faster and faster, way too fast!

He feels himself sail through the water,
Then he finds that he's falling as if the world has come to ledge.
Head over heels he falls with the water;
until in a pond of clear water he surfaces once again.

He floats around try to focus.
Try to see where he is.
When he does he sees so many trees.
He's found a new home among family and friends.

7-6-1987

6.

<u>Once A Friend Came</u>

Once a bird sang. But I didn't hear it.
I had my mind closed. I would only hear myself.

Once a child smiled. But I didn't see it.
My eyes were blinded. I would only see my frown.

Once a flower bloomed. But I didn't smell it.
I had my senses blocked. I would only smell the stench of fear.

Then …

Once a friend came,
with great wisdom.
A friend who touched me deeply,
By the strength of truth and love.

All the birds sang.
I heard them singing.
I heard those lovely songs,
from miles and miles away.

Children were playing.
I saw them smiling and laughing.
Joy overflowed as one child ran to hug me,
before I turned away.

And there were flowers blooming.
I inhaled deeply as their sweet fragrance filled the air.
This friend had gifted me her wisdom.
I now saw love and beauty everywhere ...

7-8-1987

7.

Dragonfly

I look at the world with a new perspective.
I'm not the person I was the day before.
I noticed the water down by the river,
shimmers with ripples when it reaches the shore.

As I stand here watching the ripples,
My mind starts to wonder miles away.
I can almost touch you as I see you sitting,
Your wings shinning, translucent in the morning haze.

Your head was bent in the ocean breeze,
You were a vision of heaven there in the sand.
I stood in breathless anticipation,
Unsure if you would fly off or land in my hand.

I was amazed when you flew up to me.
And softly landed in the cup my palm.
It was as if you were beckoning me,
"When I fly you should come along."

It seemed your wings fluttered in anticipation,
Their light blue beauty questioning.
As if you thought I could fly.
As if you sensed some magic in me.

But alas, my Dragonfly,
I couldn't go with you.
I shook my head; you nodded goodbye,
and then away you flew.

So now I sit beside the river.
Knowing I've been changed by my moment with you.
So many things I never noticed.
I now see the world with a dragonfly's hue.

7-8-2000

8.

<u>Autumn</u>

All the leaves are falling,
gliding gently to the ground;
in their autumn colors,
the dark oranges, reds and browns.
Just waiting to be piled up high,
for little ones to jump right in.
When the wind comes and scatters them about,
they'll rake them up and jump again.

Autumn days are perfect days.
for taking walks, and playing in leaves.
The chill in the air, the scent of cinnamon everywhere;
it's time for picking pumpkins on hands and knees.

A bon-fire and warm apple cider,
Autumn is a great time to gather with friends.
We'll bundle up when evening comes,
sitting by the fire; sharing mountain pies,
not wanting the day to end.

9-6-2015

9.
Awakened Dreams

Morning sunrise,
awakened dreams.
Quiet music,
flowing streams.

Winter weather,
Bitter chill.
Heavy silence
All is still.

Star light glowing,
sublimely bright.
Flickering fire.
warmth for the night.

9-21-1986

10.
The Mysteries of Nature

I don't seek the answers.
I seek the mysteries.
of the little things,
of tomorrow,
of life.

I seek to learn of things which go unnoticed …
Of petals of flowers,
untouched by man.
Of the pebbles of water,
hidden by sand.
Of the light of dawn's rising,
sparkling droplets of dew.
Of the birth of a fawn,
So tender so new.

9-22-1986

11.

Spirit Vision

He rides down out of the mountains on a swift Palomino.
With one strong arm he lifts me up to save my very soul.
The muddy hillside rushes down upon us with the harshness of a river.
The first of many times he saves me. This Angel as yet unknown.

Deep dark eyes, they hold the wisdom of many generations.
A young boy with the strength of many men.
His every movement is the grace of an Eagle.
The gentle ways of my Spirt friend.

Again I see him. He dances to honor the People,
the Ancient Ones.
Eagle feathers flow in the breezes as he moves to the rhythm
of sacred drums.
The power and beauty of the graceful eagle expressed,
through the dancing young man.
Renews my spirit to the ways of nature,
ways a few will never understand.

A young man of gentleness,
with ageless wisdom and strength.
He guided and protected me throughout my youth.
The gifts of my Spirit friend.

5-23-1988

12.

Grassy Fields

Children with wide happy eyes,
playing in grassy fields.
Exploring and adventurous,
content in their own little world.

Children laughing in the afternoon sun,
chasing puppies and butterflies.
Creating their own little games,
not a care, as the days go by.

Children running around on rainy days,
playing in puddles and splashing everywhere;
blowing bubbles,
and popping them before they rise in the air.

Children, enjoying themselves in grassy fields,
playing together all day long;
still laughing as the day winds down,
and catching fireflies when twilight comes.

6-2-1988

13.
Wind Blows

In summer the wind blows,
even when it's hot outside.
You can feel the heat in the breeze,
as it blows sand in your eyes.

You can see it in the movement of water,
When lakes and rivers flow swift.
You can feel it as you relax by the lakeside,
enjoying the evening mist.

In Autumn the wind is usually calmer,
just adding a bit of chill now and then.
It's nice for front porch sitting,
after harvests of crops are brought in.

In winter the wind is fierce.
Everything is laid barren and cold.
The wind buries everything green,
under heavy drifts of fresh fallen snow.

Then comes the spring time,
when the wind brings a welcomed warm breeze.
It's just right for planting seeds in the garden,
or sharing stories under nice shady trees.

3-16-1982

14.
My Woodland Home

My woodland home is hidden in a quiet meadow,
where the forest creatures and I can run free.
My cabin is lit from sun up above,
It's sheltered from storms by huge aged trees.

I rarely get visits from strangers;
but I am never alone.
The deer and other creatures are welcomed here.
It's quite crowded my little home.

3-20-1983

15.
Spring Song

In the Spring the birds all sing,
It's such a magical beautiful thing.

The symphony of spring song.
The awakening of life and nature sings along ...

The branches swing and the leaves sway,
keeping time while the rabbits play,
the rabbits thump their drumming feet,
while the crickets chirp a tune so sweet.

The lullaby of spring song soothes the babes at rest.
All the worlds falls soundly asleep,
as the birds serenade from their nests.

The magical beautiful spring song,
brings sweet dreams to the wee ones,
as the Angels sing all night long.

4-14-1982

16.
Standing, Wondering

Standing still beneath the oak tree,
watching the branches sway.
Wondering as the birds take flight,
what if I could fly that way?

Where would the breezes take me?
Would I ride the wind, drift on and on?
Or would I fly south like a winter fowl,
seeking warmth from the southern sun?

Breathing in the morning air,
as sun light warms my face.
Wondering would it warm my soul,
if I found that sun-kissed place.

Would I feel free there soaring the sky,
or with sand beneath my toes?
Or would I stand in the sun wondering,
if it's still calm under the oak tree back at home?

4-19-2006

17.
Welcome

Welcome to the forest.
Please feel free to roam a while.
But be mindful of the little ones
who always scurry about.

Many wee ones live and play here,
in borrows underground.
The chipmunks and the field mice,
are known to run around.

Be still and patient while you are here,
and maybe you will see,
a deer or two wondering by,
or a few squirrels climbing trees.

Welcome are those,
who need a little quiet,
a place to rest for a moment or two.
Welcome to our humble forest,
where you will find peace and solitude.

9-16-2011

18.
To View the Moon

I like to go out and gaze at the night sky,
to lay back in the grass and look at the moon.
I'll spread out a blanket just after sunset,
when the moon is full, and just take in the view.

I love it when the moon is so full,
that it's reflection on water lights up the sky.
When it's so bright outside there are no dark corners,
behind trees and rocks for shadows to hide.

The moon and tide are always changing,
So it's nice to stop and just watch for a while.
Feel the breeze as the tide rolls in,
and see the man in the moon as he smiles.

It's good to feel small sometimes,
as I sit under the wondrous night sky.
To lose myself to the vastness of it all,
as I gaze at the moon by the oceanside.

9-24-2014

19.

Island Waterfall

Water falls, droplets spiraling past lush foliage thick and green,
over glistening rocks, to a crystal pool; sixty feet below it seems.

Sitting on a boulder at the edge of the pool,
The spray of falling water is refreshingly cool.

The pounding roar of the falling stream,
is a rhythmic vibration, deafening to me.

There is a slippery path that leads to the top.
I contemplate climbing to measure the drop.

Using vines and roots the ensure the way.
The hike up the path is easily made.

From this vantage point, to view the sea,
I understand why the water falls; to be set free.

Water falls, free falling, swirls and pools for a while;
then continues on in a gentle current, always ocean bound.

8-4-2003

20.

Cucumber Falls

There is a place I call my sanctuary,
nestled in the Pennsylvania hills.
I hope to get back there someday,
Though sometimes I wonder if I ever will.

The water there is almost healing.
It has a glacial quality even on the hottest of days.
Wade though the creek for an hour or two,
and aches and worries just melt away.

It's a tropical climate in the middle of the mountains,
a place to escape and relax for a bit.
Every time I go back, I'm rejuvenated,
and I wonder again why I ever left.

It is my sanctuary.
I've made so many memories there.
A small glimpse of heaven in the Laurel Highlands.
An understated wonder, a beautiful Falls in the clear mountain air.

7-7-2016

21.
Finding Beauty in the Storm

The way the wind blows through the fields,
making them roll like ocean waves.
There is so much beauty here,
even on stormy days.

The way the swollen streams create waterfalls,
after torrential rains;
there is always beauty to be found,
even after a hurricane.

The way the clouds form, moving ever faster,
in darker shades of blue;
there is beauty in the storm,
even before rays of sunlight start breaking through.

Stand in the stillness as nature prepares to unleash her furry.
Breathe in the electric scent of moisture in the air,
find the beauty in the wind and the rain.
and remember as you sit in a darkened shelter,
there will always be beauty waiting out there.

7-7-2016

Night, Night, Fairy Song

Night, night. Sweet dreams.
Angel kisses and pleasant things.

Don't let the Fairies carry you,
too far into the night.
Just drift with them a while,
in the soft moon light.

Night, Night. Sweet sweet one.
Lay down your head, the Faeries are home.

Rest soundly now,
as the night grows long,
lulled by the gentle fairy song.

1-13-2013

About the Author –

Rebecca A. Baisden is an American poet.
She was born and raised in Monongahela, Pennsylvania.
As the wife of a Commercial Truck Driver she has been to many different places within the Eastern United States.
She resettled in the Tennessee Valley Area of Northern Alabama to be closer to her first grandchild in 2014.

She has been writing poetry for over thirty years.
She was first published in an anthology published by the National Library of Poetry, titled Tears of Fire in 1994.
She is the author of one other book titled Moments and Memories.

She is an active conservation volunteer and an amateur photographer.
When she is not writing or volunteering she enjoys exploring the outdoors with her family and 4 Chihuahuas near her home in Alabama.